AF654722

Duality Of Man

Omnipotent, Omniscient, Omnipresent, Omnibenevolent

Terriq

BookLeaf Publishing
India | USA | UK

Made with ❤ on the BookLeaf Publishing Platform
www.bookleafpub.in
www.bookleafpub.com

Dedication

To the divine potter, who shaped my words from the clay of my soul. And my wife Leslie, who supports me through all.

Preface

From my earliest days, I was immersed in the cadence of religious teachings, the rhythms of faith shaping the landscape of my youth. This foundation, coupled with a lifelong fascination for the power and nuance of language, led me to a profound realization: the human experience is a battlefield, an arena where unseen forces clash and contend for our very souls.

This book, then, is born from a desire to chart a course through this internal conflict. It is a chronicle of my own shortcomings, a candid exploration of the trials that mark the journey of manhood. But more than a mere catalog of failings, it is a testament to the solutions found through faith, a guidepost illuminating the path toward salvation.

Through the medium of spoken word, I endeavor to articulate a portion of this unseen war, to give voice to the struggles that often remain unspoken. It is my hope that these verses will serve as a beacon, a source of solace and strength for those who navigate the same turbulent waters. Within these pages, you will find not only the echoes of my own battles, but also the resounding truth of a guiding light, a salvation that transcends the limitations of our earthly existence.

Acknowledgements

1. The Beginning

In the beginning was the Word, and the Word was with God, and the Word was God.

There's a common theme throughout the Bible, that no matter what you read, to God be the glory. There's common traits that are displayed that show us obedience and faith can cause God to not only give, but to take—take away what does not belong, take away what distracts us and moves us in places where we may do wrong.

But God, does He give. Gives us peace of mind and a spirit that's calm, gives us a place to rest and protects us in His very palms. He guides and watches over us enough that I know when the going gets rough, we're equipped. I mean, look at Noah and the ship—that's preparation. Look at Moses and the ten commandments—that's dedication. There's already laws and regulations; all they need is obedience. I mean, look at David and Goliath—that takes faith in the mission given.

These qualities that you will read again and again, passed along from generation to generation, we should have a conversation with God, daily submission, greater patience. His teachings showed me that I can stand against giants or sit with lions with preservations. A real shepherd to guide us in the darkness, the ultimate artist. The passion He's displayed was neither cold nor lukewarm, the farthest. His lessons were like nuggets of wisdom, dropped from a place of concentration. We say thank you, Jesus, to You from Your humble servant.

2. His way

I've watched them kneel, praise rising, for the things they hold, their earthly prizes,
Yet in the same breath, a whisper, "There's better," a shadow of veiled disguises.
Through youthful eyes, I saw the truth, a chilling, stark display,
Those cherished things, those fleeting joys that God could just... take away.
"Why, Lord?" I'd plead, the question raw, that echoed through my days,
A haunting query, lingering still, in life's perplexing maze.
Blind to the path, the sacred route, the wisdom He conveys,
I clung to man's flawed, twisted views, their self-constructed graves.
But failed to view His holy way
A truth since ages past, a lesson fiercely told,
Like spirits banished, finding homes, their emptiness unfolds.
A house swept clean, yet vacant still, invites a darker sway,
Seven demons, more wicked still, to claim that empty space

But if you fill that sacred space, with Yahweh's holy light,
No vacant rooms for shadows deep, no claim to the endless nights.
No cluttered hearts, with old desires, when new grace lights the way,
For God's own presence fills the soul, and bids the darkness, "Stray!"
If faith is weak, and doubt takes hold, and shadows lead astray,
Return to words of ancient truth, and humbly, deeply pray.
For in His word, a path revealed, a beacon to obey,
To understand His sacred way, and walk with Yahweh, till this day

3. Burning

Pestilence.

A heart filled with frustration, I'm laced.
This world that we inhabit, a wasteland, made of desolation and waste.
A non-combatant.
Love and kindness, as fugitives, chased.
Resistance, their words, bitterly placed.
Formerly graced.

Warring institutions.
Cohabitation, inspirationally embraced.
Breathless, I watch as the youths' minds become displaced.
Words fall to depressions; lies and desperation, the truth has been erased.
Trust shattered, and it's been poisoned without a trace.
Tides turn into oceans.
Victims turn into graves, and the people refuse to listen.
Vicious cycle, man inside the system, displaced.

Protests that go unseen.
Anger in visions, they've embraced every head-on collision.

They won't slow until it's all been taken, the truth
between a hard place, and something's still missing.
She's angry.
He's angry.
Don't poison the children.
Deaf ears on the wicked.
What have they drunk, and what haven't they been
drinking?
World sinking.

Who's meant to be saved? A lifeboat that Noah's
building, but the faith it takes to be one of the chosen.
Dreams are for the living.
Defiance, dying, my soul has been ungiving.
I'm praying for your redemption.
I'm praying you pay attention.
I'm praying you heed instructions.
Hands, crying.
Lines drawn, time and space.
Dusk to dawn.
God's grace.
Doubts linger.
One last struggle, but still I chase.
In faith I'll follow until I finally find my place.

4. Forgiveness

Do chills, my Quest, true worship's essence hold,
Or praise, like spice, a tale yet to unfold?"
For raves, like fleeting blooms, a false embrace,
Have I, my King, confined Thy boundless space?
A charge, when faint, from earthly sockets spun,
Thy presence questioned, yet dark deeds are done?
Is Heaven's gate, from shadowed depths, a flight?
Thy nail-pierced hands, in veiled and sacred night.
That Bond, like breath of dawn, my spirit's wine,
'Pierced for my sins,' Thy wounds, a grace divine.
When prayers arise, what honeyed feelings bloom?
Does time, like myrrh, dispel my heart's dark gloom?
No glass reflects, transgressions' bitter stain,
Save in Thy form, where hidden truths remain.
Songs, like the dove's soft call, my feet they lead,
To gather flocks, where shadows darkly breed.
A Child, a lamb, with world's vast weight to bear,
By hands that formed, a mystery beyond compare.
Slashed by the healers, mocked by scornful eyes,
'Forgive them, Father,' where deep sorrow lies.
I grieve the thorns, the crimson, bitter tide,
To free my soul, where secret springs abide.
That Power on the cross, a lily's pure release,
'It is finished,' where captive spirits cease.

Peace, my beloved,' Thy tender whispers fall,
'As Father sent me,' to answer every call.
'Why troubled, now? Why doubts your spirit tease?'
'My hands, my feet,' where hidden comfort sees.
Touch me, my dove,' flesh, bone, I still remain,
John three sixteen's grace, to cleanse each earthly stain.
'For God so held the world,' His Son He gave,
That all who trust, in hidden gardens save.

5. Faint hope

Oh tender breeze that once brought somber relief.
Now Carries my hopes and scatters my very dreams.
I beseech thee the words once spoken upon me.
Travel straight and travel true like an arrow from the quiver of my belief's.
Life is but a fleeing butterfly
Flapping its frail wings.
Delicate yet strong enough to change the world which we swing.
Feeble yet fast enough to create miracles from the prayers that we sing.
Carry with you my echo, my very soul, my ethos
As you range from yonder mountains
To gaping valleys.
My hopes.
My dreams.
My tender breeze.

6. Hear ye, hear ye

Hear ye, hear ye! What price for your soul's release?
Can borrowed faith bring you everlasting peace?
Who charts your course, when grace has paved the way?
Who paints the dawn, and banishes the day's decay?
Mere words of praise, a fleeting, empty sound and space
True prayer's a fire, where grace can be found in haste
God's gifts you trade, for fleeting, earthly gain?
Then play the part, a hollow, staged refrain.
By grace you're born, a new creation's art,
No tepid faith, but passion, fire, and heart.
No shades of gray, but truth's resplendent ray,
For grace abounds, and banishes the darkest days.
Hear ye, hear ye! What vision do you seek?
To see, believe, and let your spirit speak?
Why toil in chains, when freedom's song is as clear as can be?
The world's allure, a whisper in your ear.
Counting coins, while blessings slip the air,
A soul adrift, at the close of every day.
You read the Word, yet untouched the truth remains,
Two masters serve, a soul forever lean.
No slave you are, but heir to realms above,
Released from bonds, by God's redeem.
Hear ye, hear ye! My words, a solemn plea,

Not tales of old, but truth for you and me.
Who parted seas, now calls your soul to rise,
To seek His face, with yearning, open eyes.
I pray like saints, of ages long before,
"Accept my praise, and open every door."
Faith's unseen hand, a guiding, steady light,
No earthly guide, but Spirit's pure delight.
Fill us, cleanse us, grant us full release,
Your power alone, brings our souls such peace.
Take our frail hands, and plant a seed of grace,
Psalm four eight's peace, in this appointed space.
Amen, and praise.

7. Savior

I'm not a prophet so I won't prophesize
But once I realized that the truth cannot hide I just couldn't sit beside
Because May as I try
I just couldn't waste my time
I picked up the pen because it's mightier than the sword, write ⊠⊠
I learned the word of God because I simply wanted more sight 👀
Now what I have read has shaken me to the core like
A figure from lore fright
But every word I read draws me closer to the Lords light. 💡
It's not an excuse to be afraid of dark nights
Because prayers beam through the sky and call upon our father like the dark knight.
But with these words that are curated over time, based on scriptures preserved as our life lines Im set out to remind thine that the blind can't lead the blind.
Remember Matthew 15 when Jesus replied
"Every plant that my heavenly Father didn't place will be uprooted, leave them alone
They are blind guides
And if the blind guide then blind both will fall into a pit"

I feel like Many read that but just didnt let it sit
So allow me help the masses to get further equipped.
Second Timothy chapter 3
Says every script...ture
Is inspired by God and is profitable for teaching, rebuking, correcting, and training in righteousness
So that the man of God may be thoroughly equipped for every good work.
It seems like hu-mans are always in some kinda mess
And God has already sent an example with hest a solution but people keep asking if their life is a test?
Imagine the confu-sion when you cry thinking your life went left
but God said you're now in a posi-tion
To do your absolute best
But we must be too busy chasing a check.
Say this with your chest
"For God so loved the world, that he gave his only begotten Son, that whosoever believeth in him should not perish, but have everlasting life."
Now Let that hang over you head like a spiritually tent
And I wish you the best
Now together...Amen

8. Souls design

Answers will not come easily, but yet we sneakily think that we can pull the wool over our own eyes and intercede on things that were never given willingly; like stumbling upon the ability to write songs or scribe poetry. Put your pain into your crafts like "woe is me," but forget that fruits don't bear from a barren tree. Don't miss the true meaning behind the analogy, because we were seeking deep; the son of God said, "when you're weary, come to me."

We seek the answers, yet we play the fool, thinking our lies can bend the golden rule. We claim the gifts, like songs from empty air, forgetting seeds need soil, and roots need tender care. Our pain we weave, in self-pity's disguise, ignoring grace that falls from open skies. The weary heart, a haven it can find, in arms outstretched, where love and mercy bind.

We seek answers, yet create these signs. We follow others, despite the Bible's warning to not form a line behind the blind. The world being a jungle, and us without a vine, God promises his yoke is easy, and his burden light. We can't continue in darkness when our soul was designed to shine.

9. Church

You wonder why you
Let your eyes do more talking than your presence can.
We condemn the Bible, but fail to reprimand our fellow man.
Galatians 6:1: "Brothers and sisters, if someone is caught in a sin, you who live by the Spirit should restore that person gently."
The church should be your safety,
The Bible is your certainty.
So certainly, you should be able to set your mind at ease.

If doubt and fear begin to seize,
And worldly whispers never cease,
Seek solace in the sacred plan,
Where love redeems the fallen man,
And faith provides an everlasting peace.

Proclaim that your thoughts be yours again.
We all struggle, stumble, and understand.
No one needs a dictator or someone constantly screaming they're holier than,
But a comrade, a tender friend.
Proverbs says that iron sharpens iron,
And a brother or sister is needed in the end.

Let wisdom’s light your spirit mend,
Where broken hearts find strength to transcend.
Through trials faced, on which depend,
A bond of grace, that knows no trend,
And solace found, when shadows bend,
A faithful guide, until life's send.

10. *break* love[her]

Beauty is in the eyes of the beholder, but the way I feel when I hold her, even the blind could picture your appeal.
Like a beam that's been built into a building, you've bored through me despite my heart being yours for the steal.
Words fall to impossible depths; even if it meant going to the Netherworld, I'd fall to my death if I could stare into your eyes until I draw my last breath, and I still wouldn't heal.

I could recognize you in the darkness just by your silhouette;
Even if you were mute and I were deaf,
I'd still be able to find your essence from the moment you'd taken your first steps.

In another lifetime,
Different bodies,
Different timelines,
I would love you until the last star shined, burned into the abyss.
I could land mine, fall unto, and implode into shorelines, so when the water meets the horizon, the salt from the

sea that I would still taste on your lips would send me back to the first time I met you and experienced pure bliss.

11. Wisdom

We stand at the edge, where fear and faith meet,
Afraid of the waves, the journey's defeat.
"A ship's safe at shore," a wise friend once sighed,
"But that's not its purpose," where dreams often hide.
The floodwaters rise, a man on his roof,
"God save me," he cries, seeking divine proof.
But help comes in boats, then a chopper's descent,
He refuses each hand, on heaven intent.
"How often," God asks, "must I knock at your door?
Disguised as a chance, you stubbornly ignore?"
We cling to the known, the path we can see,
And miss the grand vistas, of what life could be.
"Let dead bury dead," a wise proverb's call,
"Man lives not by bread," lest he stumble and fall.
We fixate on missteps, our eyes on the ground,
And miss the horizons, where wonders abound.
A farmer once sowed, a lesson we learn,
Some seeds found rich soil, where blessings return.
But some hit the rocks, where roots couldn't creep,
And some choked by thorns, where ambitions sleep.
So clear your own heart, like fertile terrain,
Where faith takes its hold, and washes the pain.
Remove the sharp thorns, the doubts that impede,
And blossom like fields, where new harvests you'll seed.

12. Ambivalent

What is good?

Patience is good.

Enjoying life is good.

Action is good.

Wisdom is good.

God is good.

What is bad?

Evil intentions are bad.

Action without thought is bad.

Wisdom is bad.

As written in Proverbs, loving wisdom will bring you peace, and holding onto such wisdom will bring you joy. As written in Ecclesiastes, expanding your wisdom exponentially will bring you nothing but great sorrow.

Learning how unjust the world is will scar your heart, but having an understanding of the Bible and being wise enough to seek God will cause you to seek for grace, because God is wisdom, but God is also understanding.

God's will.

If ye be in faith, it's God's will.

If something bad happens, it's God's will.

If something good happens, it's God's will.

If nothing happens, it's God's will.

If anything and everything happens, it's God's will. If someone you love lives, it's God's will.

If someone you love dies, despite convenience, it's God's will.

God's will is absolute, but because of such things, you should live life while you can, because God has only given us a few moments on this earth, and it is a sin to be foolish intentionally and waste that precious time, because a fool's actions bring nothing but destruction, and a fool's words bring great confusion unto those that are foolish enough to listen. But be a foolish man or be a wise man, every man, all men, end up back to the soil of the earth, for that is where we originate. Despite the same intentional end, there is another end, for which it makes it wise to live your life the way you want but to respect God's wishes and fear his power, for no man has more power than God, for everything your eyes gaze upon is his creation.

13. Accuse

I've been feeling highly unmotivated, deeply in depression.
It's the recession of common sense and hidden emotions that has me obligated to even break even with all my demons.
Give and take some basic information: deep sleep and early morning praying without good dreaming makes it complicated.
I'm undercompensated for just living; it's not a blessing;
A curse given naturally, born into this time-consuming and ever-growing endless life I'm living, given second chances.
My heart keeps breaking when it's inconvenient. Hold a candle to my skin and let it drip like nitrogen. On my knees, it's all I ever see whenever I have a dream: just angels fighting, running, people screaming, demons chasing, and the world burning, it seems, that i need a reconnection.
For when I read that he bleeds my needs end up in a recession.
Sunday service says we're freed but I can't find the mention.
Corinthians speaks on seeds while my mind races to top speeds and less than good deeds. Can't sleep and

hijacked dreams, but at peace when I speak and say get behind me, get thee with the same authority God left with me.

14. Fragile

Glass breaks;
you think anger is the answer to heartache.
It takes;
Love and patience, the two opposing forces of hate.
Pain isn't something that money can really erase.
When you die, how can the judge, with eyes that peirce the soul, unlatch the pearly gates and make a broken spirit whole?
"It's fate",
we've come up with so many words that mask that Gods great.
"It's fake",
We've come up with so many words that alludes that Gods great.
Morally shocked state when you realize it's too late to change ways, why do you need a chaser when lies bitter poison you willingly intake?
Numbed face and wallowing in disgrace and yet his grace resonates and keeps you standing up straight.
Yet you fail to see what's at stake so you get mad and;
Glass breaks;
You think crying is the answer to headaches;
It takes.
Commitment, Your past actions are apart of the cross

that has weight.

The heart makes Promises your body can't keep safe,

"It's late",

We've come up with so many excuses to not place.

Our trust in he who creates

Mister or Miss, take,

Up what you've let gather dust for too long;

You've prolonged.

We all.

Once thought.

That we're simply not strong.

bound to make mistakes

And you're not wrong

But through God's son

We can have faith in he whose made the way for so long.

15. Brave and Bold

People just started to realize
real eyes. realize. real lies and I cannot deny that the revolution will probably be televised.
But who am I to say that streamlined media isn't a drug that messes with our spiritual life?
When you have access to the internet at your finger tips and every piece of information takes away just a little bit, similar to how African Americans picked cotton while there slave owners took little sips and when we finally woke up and
noticed it, we were on a sinking ship so we patched up holes instead of jumping out it.
Now stands the United States of America on back breaking blacks and immigrants and it's simply amazing
Isn't it?
Broken dreams and unfulfilled promises.
Where does the world look when nobody commits?
When does senseless violence rationalize to undermine our enemy's down the line?
When do we finally awake to our pride and realize that each one of us is a lion when we don't lie
Knowledge is power, and the Bible says the righteous are as brave as lions
We serve a calling higher

It's to open real eyes, to realize the real lies,
And instead of patching holes, we rise and claim our promised skies.

16. Frigid

Frozen in place i let my fears overtake.
I fear I've overshared with my peers and along the shore lines I've lost promises that were never meant to break.
My feet stuck in the sand and panic washes over me like crashing waves.
I've apologized so many times for times I thought I made mistakes but the sun didn't rise to signify a brighter day
Yet the wind blows and my skin cracks and breaks as ice forms along my veins.
My love for the sea is replaced by hate,
My families needs feel like an endless weight which fumes the flames
The endless sea
Leaves an unsatisfactory taste
Is this the end of me?
I unilateral state, but but I've walked out here simply to get away and now my memories betray me like a dog whose owner ties him to a tree miles away
My anxiety acts like plates
Several in each hands as my mind begins to face, in prayer I hesitate and in life i wait, maybe it's too late?
The silence is piercing yet screams louder than the waves.

17. Let it be said

He who endures displays resilience
Coals that suffer flames shine with brilliance
He who lies blatantly displays defiance
Blemishes form on those who allow it
Lacking knowledge isn't a sin but wielding it for your
earthly desires makes demons your clients
Whose name do you cast them out in?
Don't be foolish for a fools errands lead them to despair
The enemy has had a millennia to plan with care
But he who relys on God knows that Allah is here
The spirit of fear isn't a seed sowed
But God lifts you up despite temperaments low

18. Unity

Unfazed
Undaunted
Undeniable
Unbreakable
Unstoppable
Unforgetting
Unforgettable
Unlikely to leave you uncertain
Unaware of the unbelievable
You've been unhappy
Feeling unseen, unheard, uneasy
But I assure you it's unwise to leave the story untold
So listen to the Universal entity
As he unzips and unwinds
Your mind to the uncanny
Unilaterally understood we stand united with our
Undaunted Lord
Our father

19. Yahweh

I lean on you in times too hard to comprehend
You give me inspiration and love that sets me apart from the mentally the world brings
You give me courage in weakness
And the voice to sing your praises
You've been my rock and salvation through struggles and tribulations
The rain may poor but you keep me pure
The wind may storm but you keep me warm
You've been the voice of reason, shielded me against formed weapons
My rod and my staff against the wicked
Yahweh the breath of life you've left within
My morning
My night
My father who art in heaven.

20. Greetings

A gentle greeting, soft and true,
"Grace and peace be with you," friends anew.
May blessings rain, a Sun rays on on your sundays,
The Lord's own favor, time cannot erase.
May God's great love, a sheltering embrace,
Surround your hearts within this earthly space.
"God bless you," whispered on the breeze,
Until we meet, like branches of the trees,
Connected by the root of saving grace.
May the Lord's kind gaze, a beacon in the night,
Shine softly down upon your home's fair gate.
And "God speed" onward, bathed in holy light.

21. Farewell

I've seen men fall to their knees, but for the wrong reasons.
I've seen people receive what was meant for others in the wrong season, but who are we to determine what anybody is worth and how long they've been waiting?
Humans and entitlement go hand in hand, yet God views us as seconds and children who merely lack the common sense to fully comprehend and understand.

We view time as a limited construct, but God sees the righteous as eternal and instructs proper conduct, yet we can't find the time to attempt it despite a lack of time and zero sense of repentance.
We repeat the same thing over and over, hoping for another ending, although we still manage to stumble over our own sentence.
Our end is only the beginning and judgment.

Do you truly belong in the kingdom when you couldn't hold down the fort or double-check the commandments?
The law has been fulfilled, and with it, completion. The Son of Man is risen, and blessings and good tides are imminent, so prepare while you can and love thy neighbor as you would any good friend.

The end.